# FROM STREETS TO STRENGTH: A Year on the Edge: An Inspiring Memoir of Overcoming Homelessness and Hardship (Books on social issues - Personal Memoirs)

A Memoir of Struggle, Strength, and Beating the System That Failed Me (Personal narratives of hardship)

Taylor Grant

## Author's Note:

*For privacy reasons, the author's name has been changed. The experiences shared in this book are deeply personal and reflect real events, emotions, and struggles. While names and certain identifying details have been altered to protect privacy, the reality of this journey remains unchanged. My hope is that by sharing this story, I can bring awareness, understanding, and hope to those who need it most.*

Part 1
# Descent into Chaos

Chapter 1
# The Moment Everything Fell Apart

The eviction notice was taped to my apartment door, its bold letters stark against the chipped paint: **"Notice to Vacate: 7 Days."** My heart raced as I read it, the weight of impending displacement pressing down on me. I had known this was coming—three months behind on rent, savings depleted—but the finality of the notice made it real in a way I wasn't prepared for.

Inside, the apartment was a testament to my dwindling existence. The once cozy space had become barren: a mattress on the floor, a rickety chair, and a small duffel bag containing my remaining possessions. The walls, which had witnessed countless memories, now seemed to close in, amplifying my sense of loss.

I reached for my phone, hands trembling, and dialed my sister's number. She answered on the third ring.

"Hey, it's me," I began, my voice unsteady. "I... I got the eviction notice today."

There was a pause. "I'm so sorry," she said softly. "I wish I could help, but with the kids and the house being so small..."

"I know," I replied, forcing a smile she couldn't see. "I just needed to tell someone."

After hanging up, I sat in silence, the reality of my situation settling in. I had no job, no savings, and now, no home. The safety net I once believed in had unraveled, leaving me dangling over an abyss of uncertainty.

That evening, I packed what little I had into my duffel bag. Each item was a fragment of my former life: a worn-out novel, a faded photograph, a threadbare sweater. As the sun dipped below the horizon, I took one last look at the apartment—a place that had been my sanctuary—and stepped out into the unknown.

The first night was the hardest. I wandered the streets, the cityscape transforming into an alien world under the cloak of darkness. Every shadow seemed menacing, every sound amplified. I found a dimly lit park and settled onto a bench, pulling my jacket tighter against the biting cold.

Sleep was elusive. The bench was unforgiving, and the noises of the night kept me on edge. I was acutely aware of my vulnerability, the stark reality of homelessness crashing over me. This was a world I had never imagined inhabiting—a world where the simple act of closing one's eyes felt like a leap of faith.

As dawn approached, I watched the city stir to life, commuters bustling to their destinations, oblivious to the invisible struggles around them. I felt a pang of isolation, a sense of being unseen in a world I once belonged to.

In the days that followed, I learned the harsh truths of survival. Public restrooms became a refuge for basic hygiene; libraries offered a warm place during the day. I discovered the unspoken territories of the homeless community—places to avoid, spots that were safer. The camaraderie among those in similar situations was both comforting and disheartening; it was a brotherhood born of desperation.

One evening, as I sat outside a convenience store, an older man approached me. His clothes were tattered, and his face bore the lines of countless hardships.

"First time out here?" he asked, his voice raspy.

I nodded.

He sat beside me, offering a half-smile. "It's tough, but you'll learn. Just keep your head up and stay aware."

His words, though simple, carried weight. They were a reminder that while I had lost my home, I hadn't lost my humanity. There was a community here, an unspoken bond among those who had fallen through the cracks.

As weeks turned into months, I adapted to this new reality. The city became both a battleground and a teacher, imparting lessons in resilience and resourcefulness. I learned which shelters were the safest, which soup kitchens served the best meals, and how to navigate the complex web of social services.

But amidst the struggle, there were moments of grace. A stranger offering a warm meal, a fellow homeless individual sharing a piece of valuable information, the warmth of a sunny day after a week of rain. These small acts of kindness became lifelines, reminders that even in the darkest times, humanity persisted.

Reflecting on that first night, I realized it was a turning point—a baptism by fire into a world I had never known. It stripped away the superficial layers of my existence, forcing me to confront my vulnerabilities and strengths. In losing everything, I began to understand the true essence of survival and the indomitable spirit that lies within us all.

Chapter 2
# The First Lessons of the Street

The initial shock of homelessness had barely settled when the pressing need for survival took over. Each day presented a new challenge, and the city, once familiar, now felt like an uncharted territory filled with hidden perils and unspoken rules.

**Finding a Place to Sleep**

Securing a safe place to sleep became my foremost concern. The park bench from my first night was neither safe nor sustainable. I quickly learned that visibility could be dangerous; being out in the open made one a target for harassment or worse. Through observation and discreet conversations, I discovered spots that offered more concealment:

• **Underpasses and Bridges**: These areas provided shelter from the elements and were less frequented by passersby. However, they were often already claimed by others, and intruding could lead to confrontations.

- **Abandoned Buildings**: Some vacant structures became makeshift refuges. Entry required caution, as these places could be structurally unsound or inhabited by individuals fiercely protective of their space.

- **24-Hour Establishments**: Places like all-night internet cafes or fast-food restaurants became temporary havens. In Japan, for instance, over 5,000 individuals, known as "Net cafe refugees," utilize 24-hour internet cafes for overnight stays.

en.wikipedia.org

The key was to remain inconspicuous. Enter after dark, leave at dawn, and avoid returning to the same spot consecutively. This nomadic approach reduced the risk of being noticed or reported.

### Navigating the Homeless Community

The homeless community was a mosaic of individuals, each with their own story. Some extended a hand of friendship, offering guidance and sharing resources. I met a man named Robert, who, despite his circumstances, navigated the streets with a sense of dignity. He introduced me to a local soup kitchen and warned me about areas to avoid after dark.

friendtothehomeless.org

However, not all encounters were benign. The desperation of the streets could drive people to deceit or aggression. I learned to be cautious, to assess intentions quickly, and to trust my instincts. Sharing details about one's sleeping spot or routine could lead to theft or worse.

## The Weight of Invisibility

One of the most profound challenges was the feeling of invisibility. During the day, I wandered the city, blending into the crowds. Yet, there was an acute awareness of being unseen in a different sense. People avoided eye contact, sidestepped, or looked through me as if acknowledging my existence might make them confront a reality they'd rather ignore.

This societal invisibility was a double-edged sword. While it allowed me to move unnoticed, it also fostered a deep sense of isolation. The fear of being judged was ever-present. I became hyper-aware of my appearance, the state of my clothes, and even my posture. Public restrooms in libraries or train stations became essential stops to maintain hygiene—a small effort to cling to a semblance of normalcy and to avoid the stigma associated with homelessness.

## Safety Measures

Safety was a constant concern. Sleeping with one eye open became a literal practice. I kept my belongings minimal and always close, using my duffel bag as a pillow to deter theft. I avoided shelters after hearing stories of violence and theft within their walls. Instead, I sought out areas with security cameras or occasional police patrols, reasoning that potential aggressors might avoid such spots.

I also learned the importance of blending in. Wearing neutral clothing, avoiding eye-catching colors or logos, and maintaining a low profile helped me stay under the radar. I refrained from engaging in panhandling or activities that might draw attention, choosing instead to seek day labor opportunities or visit charitable organizations for meals.

**Building a Routine**

Establishing a daily routine provided a semblance of control amidst the chaos. Mornings were spent at the public library, a place of refuge where I could read, rest, and plan my day. Afternoons involved searching for day labor or visiting resource centers. Evenings were dedicated to finding a safe place to sleep.

This routine not only structured my day but also helped in preserving my mental health. It gave me goals to achieve, however small, and moments to look forward to. In a situation where so much was beyond my control, these self-imposed rituals became lifelines.

The streets were an unforgiving teacher. Every decision carried weight, and the margin for error was slim. Yet, amidst the adversity, I discovered a resilience within myself I hadn't known existed. The initial days were a crucible, forging instincts and insights that would prove essential in the journey ahead.

## Chapter 3
# The Daily Struggle for Basics

The initial days of homelessness were a harsh awakening to the relentless pursuit of basic necessities. Each day became a quest for food, water, hygiene, and warmth—elements of life I had previously taken for granted.

**The Fight for Food and Water**

Securing nourishment was a constant challenge. Without a kitchen or money, I relied on soup kitchens and shelters for meals. However, these resources often had limited hours and long lines, making it difficult to depend on them consistently. I learned to carry non-perishable items like granola bars when available, scavenging from convenience stores or accepting leftovers from sympathetic strangers.

Access to clean drinking water was another hurdle. Public restrooms and parks with water fountains became essential stops. I carried an empty bottle to refill whenever possible, but during colder months, many facilities shut off their water sources to prevent freezing, leaving me parched and desperate.

## Maintaining Hygiene

Personal hygiene was a daily struggle. Public restrooms served as makeshift washrooms, but their availability was unpredictable, and using them for extended periods often drew unwanted attention. I frequented shelters that offered shower facilities, but access was limited and often came with strict schedules. Laundry was a luxury; wearing the same clothes for days became the norm, contributing to a growing sense of degradation.

## Seeking Shelter

Finding a safe place to sleep was a nightly concern. Shelters were an option, but they often reached capacity quickly, and the environment could be volatile. I explored alternative options:

- **Cars**: For those fortunate enough to have a vehicle, it provided a semblance of security and shelter. However, parking laws and the risk of theft or fines made this option precarious.

- **Couch Surfing**: Occasionally, acquaintances offered a place to stay, but these invitations were rare and often short-lived, as the burden on the host became apparent.

- **Abandoned Buildings**: These structures offered shelter from the elements but came with risks of structural instability and encounters with other desperate individuals.

Each night was a gamble, weighing the risks of exposure against the dangers of secluded spots. The constant vigilance took a toll on my mental health, exacerbating feelings of anxiety and paranoia.

**The Emotional Toll of Instability**

The ceaseless instability eroded my sense of self. The lack of routine and security led to chronic stress, manifesting in insomnia and heightened anxiety. The stigma of homelessness weighed heavily, as I felt the judgmental eyes of society upon me, further isolating me from the world I once knew.

Depression became a constant companion. The struggle to meet basic needs overshadowed any semblance of hope or ambition. The future seemed bleak, and the daily fight for survival left little room for anything beyond the immediate moment.

In this relentless battle for the basics, I discovered a resilience I never knew I possessed. Yet, the cost was a profound sense of loss—of stability, dignity, and connection to the world around me.

Part 2
# The Survival Mindset

## Chapter 4
# Navigating the System

The labyrinth of social services and government assistance programs is daunting for anyone, but when you're homeless, it can feel insurmountable. Without a permanent address, phone number, or identification, accessing aid becomes a complex endeavor. The very systems designed to help often seem impenetrable, laden with bureaucratic hurdles that test one's patience and resolve.

**The Initial Foray into Assistance**

Determined to find a way out of my predicament, I approached a local social services office. The waiting area was crowded, a testament to the number of individuals seeking help. After hours of waiting, I met with a caseworker who handed me a stack of forms. Each form required detailed information—employment history, previous addresses, identification numbers—that I struggled to provide.

One of the first obstacles was the requirement for a government-issued ID. Without one, accessing services like food assistance, housing programs, or medical care was nearly impossible. However, obtaining an ID without a permanent address or proof of residence created a frustrating loop. Studies have shown that people experiencing homelessness often encounter several barriers when attempting to obtain a government ID, including the lack of a safe place to store important personal documents, making these items subject to loss, destruction, or theft.

### The Role of Social Workers

Amidst these challenges, social workers emerged as invaluable allies. They helped navigate the convoluted pathways of assistance programs, providing guidance on which services I qualified for and how to apply. Their support was crucial in deciphering the complex web of requirements and procedures. Social workers have a responsibility to address homelessness by navigating systemic barriers of social, political, and economic structures that can help stabilize homeless clients.

### Encounters with Outreach Programs

Street outreach programs also played a significant role. Outreach workers would traverse areas known to be frequented by homeless individuals, offering assistance and information about available resources. Their efforts were instrumental in connecting me with services I was unaware of, such as temporary shelters and meal programs. These programs aim to provide education, treatment, counseling, and referrals for individuals living on the streets.

## The Bureaucratic Maze

Despite these supports, the bureaucratic nature of the system often led to delays and setbacks. Appointments were scheduled weeks in advance, paperwork was frequently lost, and miscommunications were common. The process of gaining access to permanent housing is lengthy and confusing, leading many to feel disheartened.

## The Emotional Toll

The constant navigation of this system took a significant emotional toll. Feelings of frustration, helplessness, and despair were common as I faced repeated obstacles. The stigma associated with homelessness often led to being treated with indifference or suspicion, further eroding my sense of self-worth.

## A Glimmer of Hope

After persistent effort, I was eventually connected with a housing program that offered temporary accommodation and support services. This opportunity provided a stable environment where I could focus on rebuilding my life. Programs like Rapid Re-Housing aim to help individuals obtain housing quickly, increase self-sufficiency, and remain housed.

**Reflection**

Navigating the system was one of the most challenging aspects of my experience with homelessness. The intricate web of requirements, coupled with the scarcity of resources, made accessing assistance a formidable task. However, the dedication of social workers and outreach programs provided a lifeline, guiding me through the maze and offering hope in the face of adversity.

Chapter 5
# The People you Meet

Life on the streets introduced me to a diverse tapestry of individuals, each with their own story, struggles, and survival strategies. These encounters ranged from heartwarming to harrowing, shaping my understanding of humanity in its rawest form.

**Fellow Travelers**

In the early days of my homelessness, I met Robert, a former construction worker who had lost his job and home after a severe injury. Despite his circumstances, Robert maintained a positive outlook, often sharing his limited resources and offering advice on navigating the challenges of street life. His resilience and generosity provided a semblance of community in an otherwise isolating existence.

Then there was Maria, a young woman who had fled an abusive relationship. She was cautious, keeping to herself and avoiding large groups. Over time, we developed a mutual trust, looking out for each other during the vulnerable nighttime hours. Maria's story was a stark reminder of the various paths that lead to homelessness and the strength required to survive.

## Encounters with Generosity

Acts of kindness from strangers often came unexpectedly. One cold evening, as I sat outside a café trying to stay warm, a man approached and handed me a hot cup of coffee and a sandwich. He didn't ask questions or offer unsolicited advice; he simply provided warmth and sustenance. Such gestures, though seemingly small, had a profound impact, offering moments of relief and restoring faith in humanity.

Local outreach programs also played a crucial role. Volunteers would distribute blankets, hygiene kits, and information about available services. Their consistent presence provided not just material support but also a sense of being seen and valued.

## The Predators

Unfortunately, the streets were not devoid of danger. I learned quickly to be wary of individuals who sought to exploit the vulnerable. There were those who offered shelter or assistance with ulterior motives, leading to situations of coercion or abuse. Substance abuse was rampant, and some individuals would resort to theft or violence to support their addictions.

One night, I was approached by a man named Jack, who offered me a place to stay. Desperate for shelter, I accepted, only to find myself in a precarious situation where leaving became difficult without confrontation. I managed to extricate myself, but the experience left me more cautious and aware of the potential dangers lurking behind seemingly kind offers.

**Navigating Trust and Caution**

Building relationships on the streets required a delicate balance between trust and caution. While camaraderie could provide protection and shared resources, misplaced trust could lead to victimization. I learned to observe behaviors closely, rely on intuition, and establish boundaries to safeguard myself.

The fear of being seen and judged was a constant companion. Society often views the homeless through a lens of stigma, associating homelessness with personal failure or moral shortcomings. This perception led to feelings of shame and a desire to remain invisible, avoiding interactions that could result in humiliation or rejection.

The people I met during this period left indelible marks on my journey. Their stories intertwined with mine, creating a complex narrative of survival, resilience, and the human capacity for both kindness and cruelty. These interactions taught me invaluable lessons about empathy, the importance of community, and the necessity of vigilance in the face of adversity.

Chapter 6
# Who I Became in the Process

The relentless challenges of homelessness exacted a profound mental and emotional toll, reshaping my identity and worldview in ways I could never have anticipated.

**The Mental and Emotional Toll of Survival**

Each day was a battle against not only external adversities but also internal turmoil. The constant uncertainty and exposure to harsh conditions led to chronic stress, manifesting as anxiety and depression. Sleep became elusive, with the fear of vulnerability in public spaces keeping me on constant alert. This hyper-vigilance, while a necessary survival mechanism, further eroded my mental well-being.

The stigma associated with homelessness weighed heavily on me. Society's judgmental glances and dismissive attitudes fostered feelings of shame and worthlessness. I began to internalize these perceptions, questioning my self-worth and doubting my ability to reintegrate into the world I once knew.

. . .

### Learning Self-Reliance in Unimaginable Ways

Amidst the adversity, I discovered reservoirs of resilience and adaptability. Necessity became my teacher, compelling me to develop skills and strategies I had never imagined.

- **Resourcefulness**: I learned to navigate the city's landscape to find essential services, from locating public restrooms to identifying places that offered free meals. I became adept at reading people and situations, discerning where I might find assistance or where I needed to exercise caution.

- **Community Building**: Despite the transient nature of street life, I formed bonds with fellow individuals experiencing homelessness. We shared information, resources, and support, creating a makeshift community bound by shared experiences. These relationships taught me the importance of mutual aid and the strength found in collective resilience.

- **Adaptability**: The ever-changing circumstances forced me to remain flexible. Plans were often rendered obsolete by unforeseen events, requiring me to think on my feet and adjust swiftly. This adaptability became a crucial component of my survival strategy.

### The Hardest Moral Choices I Had to Make

Survival on the streets often presented moral dilemmas that challenged my ethical framework. The line between right and wrong blurred under the weight of desperation.

- **Trespassing for Shelter**: On several occasions, I faced the choice of sleeping in unauthorized areas, such as abandoned buildings or private properties. While aware that this was against the law, the alternative was exposure to the elements and potential harm. I grappled with the guilt of violating others' spaces but justified it as a necessity for survival.

- **Accepting Questionable Offers**: There were times when offers of assistance came with strings attached, leading to situations that compromised my personal boundaries. The need for shelter or food sometimes outweighed my discomfort, forcing me into morally ambiguous situations.

- **Withholding Help**: In the face of limited resources, I occasionally found myself turning away from others in need. The instinct for self-preservation overrode the impulse to assist, leading to internal conflicts and feelings of remorse.

These experiences forced me to confront the complexities of morality in survival situations. I learned that ethical decisions are often context-dependent, and actions that might be deemed unacceptable in ordinary circumstances become justifiable when one's survival is at stake.

### Emerging Transformed

The crucible of homelessness stripped away superficial layers of my identity, revealing core aspects of my character. I emerged with a deeper understanding of resilience, empathy, and the human capacity for adaptation. The experience reshaped my values, instilling a profound appreciation for stability, community, and the simple necessities of life.

While the journey was fraught with hardship, it also illuminated the strength of the human spirit. I learned that even in the face of overwhelming adversity, it is possible to find moments of grace, to forge connections, and to discover facets of oneself that remain dormant until tested by the harshest of circumstances.

Part 3

# The Breaking Point and the Climb Out

Chapter 7

# The Path to Something Better

After months of enduring the relentless challenges of homelessness, a faint glimmer of hope emerged, signaling the possibility of a way out. It began with small opportunities that, collectively, made a significant difference in my journey toward stability.

**The First Glimmer of a Way Out**

One chilly morning, while seeking warmth in a public library, I noticed a flyer pinned to the community board: "Job Fair – Opportunities for All. No Experience Necessary." The event was scheduled for the following week at a nearby community center. Despite my tattered appearance and dwindling self-esteem, I decided to attend, viewing it as a potential lifeline.

## Small Opportunities That Made a Big Difference

At the job fair, various organizations had set up booths, offering positions ranging from manual labor to entry-level office roles. One booth, in particular, caught my attention—a local nonprofit dedicated to helping individuals reintegrate into the workforce. They offered a program that provided temporary employment, skills training, and assistance with securing permanent housing.

I approached the representative, a compassionate woman named Sarah, and candidly shared my situation. She listened intently, without a hint of judgment, and explained that their program was designed precisely for individuals like me. She handed me an application and assured me that my current circumstances would not be a barrier to participation.

## The People, Moments, or Decisions That Began Shifting My Reality

Sarah's empathy and the nonprofit's inclusive approach marked a pivotal moment in my journey. I completed the application and, within a week, was enrolled in their program. They provided me with part-time work, helping to clean and maintain public parks. The job not only offered a modest income but also instilled a renewed sense of purpose.

Through the program, I met others who had faced similar hardships. We formed a supportive community, sharing resources and encouragement. The organization also connected me with a case manager who assisted in obtaining identification documents, applying for benefits, and exploring housing options.

One evening, after a particularly exhausting day, I attended a support group meeting facilitated by the nonprofit. There, I met James, a former program participant who had successfully transitioned to stable employment and housing. His story resonated deeply with me, serving as a tangible example of what was possible. James became a mentor, offering guidance and motivation during moments of doubt.

These cumulative experiences—the job fair, Sarah's kindness, the nonprofit's resources, and James's mentorship—began to shift my reality. They illuminated a path forward, demonstrating that, despite the depths of my despair, a better future was attainable.

Reflecting on this period, I recognize that it was the convergence of small opportunities and the unwavering support of compassionate individuals that reignited my hope. Each step, no matter how minor it seemed at the time, contributed to my gradual emergence from the shadows of homelessness into the light of possibility.

Chapter 8
# Climbing Out of Survival Mode

The path out of homelessness was neither swift nor linear. Every step forward seemed fragile, as if the smallest misstep could send me spiraling back. But for the first time in a long while, I was beginning to see something resembling stability.

**The Slow Climb to Stability**

I started to rebuild my life one small decision at a time. The nonprofit program had given me a crucial foothold, but I knew part-time work alone wouldn't be enough to secure long-term stability. My caseworker, Amanda, encouraged me to apply for a transitional housing program that helped people move from shelters or unstable conditions into permanent housing.

The waitlist was long, but I was lucky—my temporary job gave me a small but steady income, and that made me a priority candidate. When I finally received the call that I had been accepted into a housing program, I nearly broke down. I had been preparing myself for another rejection, another closed door. Instead, I was given a second chance.

The housing wasn't luxurious—just a small shared apartment in a transitional living space—but to me, it felt like a palace. Having four walls and a locked door for the first time in months gave me an overwhelming sense of security. I slept better than I had in ages, no longer waking up in a cold sweat, paranoid about someone stealing my belongings or being forced to move in the middle of the night.

**Relearning Normal Life**

Moving into stable housing didn't immediately erase the survival instincts I had developed. It took time to adjust to sleeping in a bed again. I still hoarded food, stuffing granola bars into my backpack in case I suddenly lost everything. I caught myself eating meals quickly, as if they might be taken away at any moment.

Social interactions were another challenge. I had spent so much time feeling invisible or judged that it was difficult to connect with people in a normal way. Making eye contact, engaging in casual conversations, and trusting others felt foreign, even forced.

But little by little, I began to reintegrate. The job program offered professional development workshops, helping me learn new skills and improve my resume. I practiced mock interviews, learning how to explain my employment gap without letting shame consume me.

Then came a breakthrough. A local hotel was hiring for full-time housekeeping staff. It wasn't glamorous, but it was steady work with benefits. I applied, half-expecting rejection, but to my surprise, I was hired. The first paycheck I received felt unreal. It wasn't much, but it was mine—I had earned it.

**The Fear of Falling Back**

Even as things improved, I remained terrified of slipping back into homelessness. I had seen it happen to others—people who had secured housing, only to lose it again after an unexpected medical bill, job loss, or landlord dispute. The system wasn't designed to catch you when you stumbled.

I became obsessive about financial planning, saving every extra dollar I could. I took on extra shifts when available, even if it meant exhaustion. My entire focus was on ensuring I never ended up on the streets again.

Still, I couldn't shake the feeling that I didn't fully belong in the world I was re-entering. Friends and coworkers talked about things like weekend vacations, home décor, and future plans. My world had been so focused on immediate survival that the idea of planning for the future felt surreal. I didn't know how to dream beyond the next month's rent.

**Looking Forward**

Despite my fears, I was slowly finding my way back. The survival mode mindset didn't disappear overnight, but each day, it loosened its grip on me.

I wasn't just surviving anymore—I was living.

For the first time in years, I allowed myself to think about what could come next. Maybe I could save up for my own apartment. Maybe I could go back to school. Maybe I could finally stop looking over my shoulder, waiting for everything to collapse again.

For so long, I had believed that once you fell into homelessness, you never truly left it behind. But I was beginning to realize that while the experience had changed me forever, it didn't have to define me.

I wasn't just climbing out of survival mode—I was reclaiming my life.

# Life After the Edge

Even after securing housing, a job, and some sense of stability, I carried the weight of my experiences with me. Homelessness doesn't just end the moment you step into a home—it lingers in your mind, in your habits, in the way you see the world. I had spent a year on the edge of survival, and that kind of experience doesn't simply disappear.

**What Homelessness Taught Me About Survival, People, and the System**

Homelessness strips life down to its rawest form. It teaches you what truly matters—safety, food, warmth, and the ability to trust. It also exposes just how fragile stability can be. Before, I had assumed homelessness was the result of a series of bad choices. Now, I knew better.

I had met people who lost everything after a medical emergency, a divorce, a sudden layoff. I had seen how one wrong turn, one piece of bad luck, could send someone spiraling into the same world I had struggled to escape. The system was not designed to catch people—it was designed to filter them out, to make them jump through endless hoops just to receive the bare minimum of help.

I learned that survival is not just about food and shelter—it's about resilience, adaptability, and the ability to keep moving forward even when everything seems hopeless. I saw the best and worst of people: the strangers who offered kindness without judgment, and the ones who looked right through me as if I were invisible.

## The Lasting Scars and Lessons from a Year on the Streets

Even now, years later, certain habits remain. I still feel uneasy when I see a police officer approaching, even though I'm no longer at risk of being told to "move along." I still catch myself hoarding small items—an extra granola bar, a bottle of water—just in case.

The biggest scar, however, is the fear. The fear that if I lose my job, if I miss a rent payment, if something unexpected happens, I could end up right back where I was. That fear never fully fades, because I know now how easily it can happen.

But along with the scars, there are lessons—lessons about resilience, about self-reliance, and about the importance of community. I know now that no one truly makes it alone. We survive because of the people who extend a hand when we are at our lowest.

· · ·

## The Invisible Homeless—Why So Many Never Find Their Way Back

For every person who escapes homelessness, there are countless others who don't. Some get trapped in the system—endless waitlists, bureaucratic red tape, shelters that are unsafe or inaccessible. Others fall into addiction or mental illness, often because the struggle to survive is so relentless that numbing the pain seems like the only option.

And then there are the ones who become invisible. They sleep in cars, couch-surf with acquaintances, or live in cheap motels. They aren't counted in official statistics, but they are homeless just the same. They are the ones working minimum-wage jobs, washing up in public restrooms before a shift, pretending they have a place to go at night. Society doesn't see them, and so they remain trapped in a cycle that never truly ends.

## A Message to Those Still Struggling: Hope, Resilience, and What Can Help

If I could say one thing to someone still living through what I did, it would be this: **You are not broken. This is not your fault. And you are not alone.**

The world may look at you as if you are invisible, but you are not. There are people who will help—not all of them, but enough to make a difference. It only takes one opportunity, one person who believes in you, to change everything.

I won't say it's easy. It isn't. Climbing out is the hardest thing you will ever do. But you are stronger than you think. The fact that you are still here, still fighting, proves that.

And to those who have never experienced homelessness, I ask this: **See us.** See the people sleeping in doorways, sitting in libraries, trying to get through another day. They are not statistics. They are human beings, just like you.

I was one of them. And I will never forget.

www.ingramcontent.com/pod-product-compliance
Lightning Source LLC
LaVergne TN
LVHW050029080526
838202LV00070B/6983